AMA Theology

by

Alan Agarrat

RB
Rossendale Books

Published by Lulu Enterprises Inc.
3101 Hillsborough Street
Suite 210
Raleigh, NC 27607-5436
United States of America

Published in paperback 2023
Category: Religious/Christian
Copyright 2023 © by Alan Agarrat
ISBN : 978-1-4477-0581-9

All rights reserved. No part of this publication may be reproduced, stored in a retrieval system or in any form by any means, without the prior permission in writing of the author, nor be otherwise circulated in any form of binding or cover other than that in which it is published and without similar condition including this condition being imposed on the subsequent purchaser.

Other books by this author:

"Truth by Alan Agarrat" (2013)

"Thoughts by Alan Agarrat" (2016)

"Kingdoms, Governments & Rulers by Alan Agarrat" (2018)

"Forward to Better by Alan Agarrat" (2022)

Satan is Laughing by Alan Agarrat (2022)

CONTENTS

Acknowledgment 7

Foreword 8

1. My Theology – (Simple) – AMA Theology 9
2. GOD is not Religious 13
3. Study of GOD 17
4. GOD Gives Talents 21
5. Male and Female 23
6. GOD Only Tells Truth 25
7. GOD Warns of Satan 27
8. GOD's Thinking Differ to Man's Ways 30
9. Differences between Belief and Knowledge .. 33
10. GOD Respects Man 37

AMA Theology

Acknowledgment

In dedication to GOD's Respect to Man.

AMA Theology

Foreword

This world is in need of GOD to transform lives.

AMA Theology

1. My Theology – (Simple) – AMA Theology

My theology is simply based on a study of GOD (ie GOD The Father). I believe that there are various "Theologies" which study religions, worship, study of the divine, the history of how religious practices came about, the protocol of how garments are to be worn, etc. I believe that the main resource for studying GOD, is the Bible.

Which reporter or person was around when the Earth was created?

AMA Theology

Nevertheless there is an account of the creation of the Earth, its seas, lands, trees, fish, birds, land animals and humans. Is there proof to show it was not so? Is the stated order of creation incorrect – for example did birds exist before cattle? Mankind are apparently searching outside this earth, to find out how life may have been created. Have we or scientists found out if the chicken came before the egg?

Now the writer of Genesis I believe is Moses. How did he know what to write? I believe Moses was inspired by GOD to state certain accounts. Present scientists carry out research and records of experiences, to determine their statements or results. Moses did not have such research. How did Moses

AMA Theology

know what to record? What school did Moses attend to get such literature?

I have not attended any establishment for learning "Theology" and cannot say that I have any great "Intellect" for divulging advance knowledge. But I hope that some of my insights have been gained from "The Holy Ghost" – by inspiration.

Theologians have given their insights to GOD, church, justification for religious practices, lack of reason for some religious post, etc. But I will like to know theologians views on their study of Satan. If theology is the study of GOD, then there should be a word for the study of Satan. Perhaps the word "Santology" may be appropriate. Persons may view/read my booklet

AMA Theology

"Satan is Laughing". In a book, it did state that this world is more consistent with an evil deity.

AMA Theology

2. GOD is not Religious

What does religious mean? Religious may entail carrying on set practices on a regular schedule. A football team supporter may be said to be "religious" in that the said person attends and/or supports his team at practically every home match. We may then ask ourselves: "What does GOD do on a regular basis?" GOD The Father has only said a few words in the New Testament basically saying: "Christ is my beloved Son, listen to him". We should note that GOD only said so, once. Similarly we

AMA Theology

note that Jesus Christ gave his Commandments once in that we are to (1) love GOD with all our minds, with all our heart and with all our souls and (2) we are to love our fellowman as ourselves.

Christ only gave the "Lord's Prayer" once and it is recited billions of times each Sunday but very, very few know how to express it in five words. The "Lord's Prayer" begins with "Our Farther who are in Heaven, hallowed be thy name." Practically everyone will not be able to tell you what is:- GOD's name. My best guess for GOD's name is: "Yahweh". It would appear that over time using this name or what was its original, was abandoned, discouraged or "frown on" because of uncertainty of

AMA Theology

its original and how was spelt and pronounced.

Unfortunately Jesus Christ never uttered GOD's personal name. We may understand why this is so, as practically all children do not call their father by their first or Christian name. Children generally say "Daddy" or "My Father".

On the other hand, has GOD got a religion? We can see that humans have many religions. Some believe as Christians, Hindi, Moslems, Buddah, "In Money and/or Wealth", Some simply belief in "Themselves".

Many believe GOD created life. But Who created death?

GOD created humans in GOD's image and likeness. Very, very few know and

AMA Theology

can state what characteristics are common to GOD and humans.

GOD said that we should have no other god but "GOD". But some go ahead with making their own religions of "themselves and/or their egos", "Money and/or wealth", etc.

Where in the Bible are the following words:

- Christmas – **(for Christ Birth)**

- Easter

- Trinity

- Jehovah

- Blackman or Whiteman

- Confession

AMA Theology

3. Study of GOD

The best way of studying GOD maybe, by what is written in the Bible rather than what others may say about HIM. An important statement one should bear in mind is that we should love GOD with our minds. We are to consider what is said in the Bible and think of the relevance to how that plays in our lives. Jesus Christ is one being who seems to have had contact with "GOD The Father", and we should take note of what Christ says about GOD. For example GOD is greater than Christ and it would appear that GOD

AMA Theology

resurrected Christ from the dead. When will Christ return to Earth, is apparently to be determined by GOD as opposed to Jesus Christ.

In the beginning of the Bible we see that GOD is a creator. Likewise, humans are also creators. Other characteristics which I believe are common to GOD and mankind, are: "feelings" and "a sense of humour". I may not give Biblical justification for these latter two traits but they may arise from my apparent communication with the Holy Ghost. Still GOD said HE is a jealous GOD and there should be no other gods but HIM. I think this shows that GOD has feelings.

One common characteristic which recently hit me, is that GOD and men,

AMA Theology

"need to rest". I have seen men enjoying themselves for an apparent endless duration, when they suddenly fall into a deep sleep.

I also now seem to think that GOD and humans have means of communicating - Something in common!

Men give examinations/tests for persons to have proper qualifications. Similarly GOD tests our lives so perhaps we may gain approval for HIS Kingdom.

Wisdom seems to be a quality which many will like to have. But there does not seem to be any human establishment which give a qualification in "Wisdom". I would say that wisdom is a gift for making the correct decisions. It is said that the fear of GOD is the beginning of wisdom. It seems that Solomon was given wisdom which no one can match or demonstrate, to this day. What made Solomon think of cutting the child in half to decide which of the two ladies was the correct mother of the child? Did he have a reference booklet for making such decision?

I cannot recall GOD or Jesus Christ referring to any individual as being a "Saint". Nevertheless men appoint some individuals as "Saints".

AMA Theology

4. GOD Gives Talents

Some people seem to have special talents and I can only assume that such are given by GOD. I may be bias as I look at some sport men – Pelé, Muhammad Ali, Wilt Chamberlain, Michael Jordan, or musicians such as Oscar Peterson or singers, Nancy Wilson and Nat King Cole - persons given special talents!

I am sure GOD has given special spiritual gifts to some persons for understanding GOD and for providing prophetic knowledge. We should think

AMA Theology

of what made some persons to write passages in the Bible.

GOD communicates especially in early days of history. HE is said to have communicated with Adam, Noah, etc. But in latter days, GOD used Jesus Christ to convey things to mankind. I also believe that after Christ's time on earth, GOD has used the Holy Ghost via individuals, to convey things to mankind.

Nevertheless we should be aware of so called "clever men" Who apparently say they are working for GOD and who often use sentences with double negatives just to confuse others. Such statements probably don't mean or say, anything of truly enlightenment.

AMA Theology

5. Male and Female

GOD created humans male and female. Therefore HE seems to appreciate there are significances in persons having gender. Mary gave birth to a son Jesus Christ, as opposed to a girl. What is the difference between males and females?

Nowadays there seems to be instances where persons are changing their sex or gender, from male to female and vice versa. Nowhere in the Bible this seems to be recorded or happen. Were such changes of sex or gender, happening

AMA Theology

centuries or hundreds of years ago? Some has the impression that we are to move with a modern attitude of having persons be liberated to be what they feel. So if someone feels they were born male and subsequently they feel they are female, then, should they be identified as being female? Similarly a person born female who subsequently feels they are male, should they be identified as male? Sometime ago, such females were referred to as "tomboys".

On the day of judgement, how will the Good Lord view such persons who have apparently changed their gender from that which they were born?

There is another situation where persons are sexually attracted to persons of the same sex or gender.

AMA Theology

6. GOD Only Tells Truth

We can test GOD to find out if HE has ever told a lie. It may be said that GOD only tells the truth and HE has a characteristic of not telling a lie. Prophets did state that GOD does not lie as seen/recorded in Numbers Ch23, v16, TitusCh1,v2 and Hebrews Ch6, v18.

GOD and through his prophets, has said things as they are and/or will be, this includes even unsavoury accounts or unpleasant events. From the beginning GOD told Adam and Eve if

AMA Theology

they partook of the forbidden tree, they will die. It is also apparent that GOD often spoke to Moses, including giving Ten Commandments.

GOD also gave signs of things/events at the latter part of man's world. As Jesus Christ stated in Matthew Ch24, v7: "For nation shall rise against nation, and Kingdom against kingdom: and there shall be famines, and pestilences, and earthquakes in divers places". We see such happenings.

Christ said that there will always be the poor.

The future will tell if things which were prophesied as told in the Bible, will come to pass. For example, we wait to see if Jesus Christ returns to the Earth.

AMA Theology

7. GOD Warns of Satan

Part of bad news especially through Jesus Christ, is GOD's warning of Satan. I find it interesting that the word "Satan" is only used once or twice in the Old Testament in Job Ch1, v6. In Zechariah Ch3, v1-2 the Lord rebukes Satan. I find it strange that Satan is not mentioned more in the Old Testament. Satan may have been implied as the serpent (a creature of a subtle or crafty nature) in Genesis Ch3, v2-4 &v13/14.

AMA Theology

Jesus Christ had some interactions and remarks with respect to Satan (otherwise referred to as the Devil or the "Wicked one"). These are related in Matthew Ch4, v1 to v11, Matthew Ch12, v26, Matthew Ch13, v19 and Matthew Ch13, v39. Matthew Ch25, v41, Jesus indicates that the Devil is not worthy of good and is of a bad unclean attitude, but that the Devil is destined for everlasting fire or Hell.

Christ also had remarks with respect to those who do Satan's work – I refer to them as "Agents of Satan". In St John Ch8, v44, Jesus told Pharisees that they were of the Devil, indicating they (ie Agents of Devil or Satan) were doing the Devil's deeds or works - The Devil being the "Father of Lies".

AMA Theology

In St Matthew C6, v38 Jesus talked of tares or the bad ones as children of the wicked one (Satan/Devil?) and these tares are sown by the Devil.

In St Matthew Ch23, v14 to v37, Jesus talked of Scribes and Pharisees as being hypocrites and they were being destined for Hell.

We are to always bear in mind that Jesus was and is, the main messenger of GOD. What Jesus says, it is as if, GOD is saying the same.

AMA Theology

8. GOD's Thinking Differ to Man's Ways

Man's or should I say human's way of thinking, is generally different to that of GOD's thinking. For example people are conditioned by what others say and do. Humans are generally indoctrinated by other humans. But who indoctrinates GOD. Many persons have the belief that Jesus Christ is the person with the greatest influence in "This World". This may be due to the teachings of religious leaders. But I believe GOD

AMA Theology

has put it in a different way by saying: "Eve is the mother of all nations" – Geneses Ch3, v20.

GOD seems to have chosen the lowly in man's society, to do great deeds or utter profound statements. For example, such words as uttered by one of the criminals who was crucified with Christ. That criminal was the only one to be given personal assurance by Christ (and I presumed with GOD endorsement) to be with Christ in the Christ's Kingdom.

Humans tend to admire the cunningness of persons whereas GOD looks at, or appreciates, the sincerity of a person's heart. St Paul in 1 Corinthians Ch3, says: "The Lord knows wise men's thoughts: HE knows how useless they are". Are we to judge or recognise how men's actions have been in effecting things on earth?

Men generally have an attitude of "self vindication" or "I told you so". GOD and through HIS prophets pre-warn of many occurrences. When such occurrences occur, GOD has nothing more to say of the happening. Or should I say: GOD does not boast.

AMA Theology

9. Differences between Belief and Knowledge

No one presently living, knows of anything that happened 150 years ago or 1,500 years ago, etc. I am of the opinion that they believe of what has happened 150 years ago, by what they have read or given pronouncement of, which may be of a dubious nature. **A person only knows of what they have personally observed.** For example, on Tuesday 28 February 2023, I observed that it was very cold at Willesden Stadium in

AMA Theology

London, such that my hands were almost frozen and I saw frost caused the grass to turn white. I know that from my senses. Now if I told a person in Australia of the said conditions. Will that person know of the said conditions or will that person believe of the said weather conditions of Willesden, as I told that person? Now if that person in Australia has confidence in my word from the fact that I have always told him the truth, **he will believe me**.

Practically everyone knows their date of birth. But do they really know of their birth or do they believe their date of birth. They were told of their date of birth and a birth certificate shows their birth date. Hopefully the certificate is correct. Can you imagine a baby at the

AMA Theology

time of their birth, knowing the date? They were told so at a later date. We are very much used to others giving us information and we trust that others are giving us correct information and facts.

We have a similar position with GOD. We can only believe that GOD exists. Our confidence in GOD, is based on what HE and Christ have said.

It is easy or should be easy to believe in a being that always tells you or conveys to you, the truth.

On Judgement Day, all will then believe GOD.

It is said that GOD created things in six days and rested on the seventh day. I believe that those six day periods were not "24 hour periods" as we now know

AMA Theology

them as the time it takes for the earth to complete a spin. It remains to be seen if GOD takes me to task for not believing "24 hour periods". Unfortunately the Bible does not say what happened on the eight of such days.

We may take such "days" as "GOD days" which are much longer than "24 hour periods".

If they were "24 hour periods", then we may assume that GOD resumed working long time ago. I do not take "assume" = "ass-u-me".

AMA Theology

10. GOD Respects Man

GOD has respect (or may I say, has love) for mankind. HE wants men to be part of a Kingdom. HE sent his son Jesus to proclaim such a Kingdom and gave guidelines for man's welfare. GOD seems to regard humans as HIS children. Parents with children should identify such feelings towards their children. Feelings that their children are taken care of, developed to be independent adults, given good advice and examples, have good moral attitudes and actions, etc.

AMA Theology

Parents do have feelings of disappointment or sorry when a child shows persistent attitudes of doing incorrect/bad things or not following their parent's guidelines.

We should aim for GOD to see us as HIS beloved children in whom HE is well pleased.

AMEN.

Printed by BoD in Norderstedt, Germany